HIDDEN FACES OF
INDIA

HIDDEN FACES OF
INDIA

PALANI MOHAN

CONTENTS

Preface

This book, a collection of nine stories about India, is the result of many years of visiting the country—as a photographer, and as an Indian.

My family left Chennai, the southern city of my birth, then known as Madras, and migrated to Australia when I was a child. But eventually, India, this most fascinating and beguiling of countries, drew me back.

Many of the people and places that appear in these pages I first knew as a young boy. Like other children I was taken with my cousins to fly kites on Marina Beach and told bedtime tales of the mighty elephants of Top Slip.

Revisiting them turned out to be a journey of personal discovery; spent peeling away the preconceptions that shroud India and mask its grandeur and humanity. More than just revisiting the past, it was about gaining a better understanding of the complexities of a country with more than 1.2 billion people and a multitude of languages and religions.

These images show a changing India, but one which is holding on tightly to its beliefs and traditions, from troubled and icy Kashmir in the north to the tranquil and balmy Tamil Nadu in the south.

During my travels I met many ordinary folk and had long conversations with them as we whiled away journeys, or sat together in their homes or in smoke-filled tea shops. They told me about their lives, what God had dealt them, and their hopes and aspirations for the future. These simple stories are something I will always treasure; they are indeed the hidden faces of India.

This is indeed India! The land of dreams and romance, of fabulous wealth and fabulous poverty, of splendor and rags, of palaces and hovels, of famine and pestilence, of genii and giants and Aladdin lamps, of tigers and elephants, the cobra and the jungle, the country of a hundred nations and a hundred tongues, of a thousand religions and two million gods, cradle of the human race, birthplace of human speech, mother of history, grandmother of legend, great-grandmother of tradition, whose yesterdays bear date with the mouldering antiquities of the rest of the nations—the one sole country under the sun that is endowed with an imperishable interest for alien prince and alien peasant, for lettered and ignorant, wise and fool, rich and poor, bond and free, the one land that all men desire to see, and having seen once, by even a glimpse, would not give that glimpse for the shows of all the rest of the globe combined.

Mark Twain

Following the Equator

1896

The Pushkar Fair

When the full moon rises over Pushkar during the Hindu month of Kartik, an unparalleled gathering of man and beast takes place on the dunes that encircle this holy city in the desert state of Rajasthan. Renowned as one of the greatest spectacles on Earth, and famous for the 80 000 camels that are traded here every year, the annual Pushkar Fair also draws thousands of ponies, buffalo and other prized livestock from villages and towns across the Thar Desert and beyond.

Pilgrims, too, arrive in their hundreds of thousands to bathe at the fifty-two ghats arrayed around the lake that sits at the centre of Pushkar, a blue jewel at the heart of the city's tangle of lanes and whitewashed shops, temples and homes. Legend has it that a dip in the waters during Kartik Purnima, the November full moon, is equivalent to performing *yagnas*, or ritual prayers, for several hundred years.

At dawn the air comes alive with the roar and grumble of bulls facing off against each other, or parading for females with an alarming display of growling and gargling. As the winter sun moves overhead the noise subsides and the makeshift camps retreat into a half-slumber bathed by the season's red-gold light. On the edge of town, resplendent in ornamental bridles and with their coats glossed to a high sheen, stand the ranks of ponies tethered by their hind feet to a complicated network of ropes, ready to be bought as a status symbol by only the richest of Rajasthan's families.

Some of the camels on show are brought hundreds of miles by professional traders, while others are led to Pushkar on foot by men who carry their whole village's hopes for a prosperous year. Most will hold out for the highest possible price, and if unsuccessful will strike out on the long journey home to wait for another fair or another year.

Judged for their beauty and temperament as much as their gait and build, it is easy to see why camels are prized above buffalos and elephants as beasts of burden in this arid state. Standing regally on the dunes or loping along the sand, the towering beasts are decorated with pompoms attached to their wooden nosepegs and bright strings of beads and bells around their necks and ankles. Auspicious symbols are daubed in black paint on their coats, which are painstakingly clipped in traditional geometric tribal shapes at makeshift barbers' shops set up alongside fodder stalls.

As the moon waxes and the religious festival reaches its height, the camels and other livestock disperse and a carnival atmosphere reigns. Jugglers, poets and acrobats vie for attention in the streets already crowded by beggars, cows, ash-smeared holy men and merchants selling all manner of brightly-coloured wares. Rows of shops offer every implement for the farm, and outside shoe stalls worn-out sandals litter the ground, discarded by the proud owners of new footwear.

As quickly as it began the festival is over, with a mass exodus of villagers who have completed their religious duties and wrapped up their business, leaving the little town to slumber for another year.

The sun rises over the livestock grounds outside the holy city of Pushkar.

Man and beast drink from the same water supply.

Herds of unsold camels begin the long journey back to their villages.

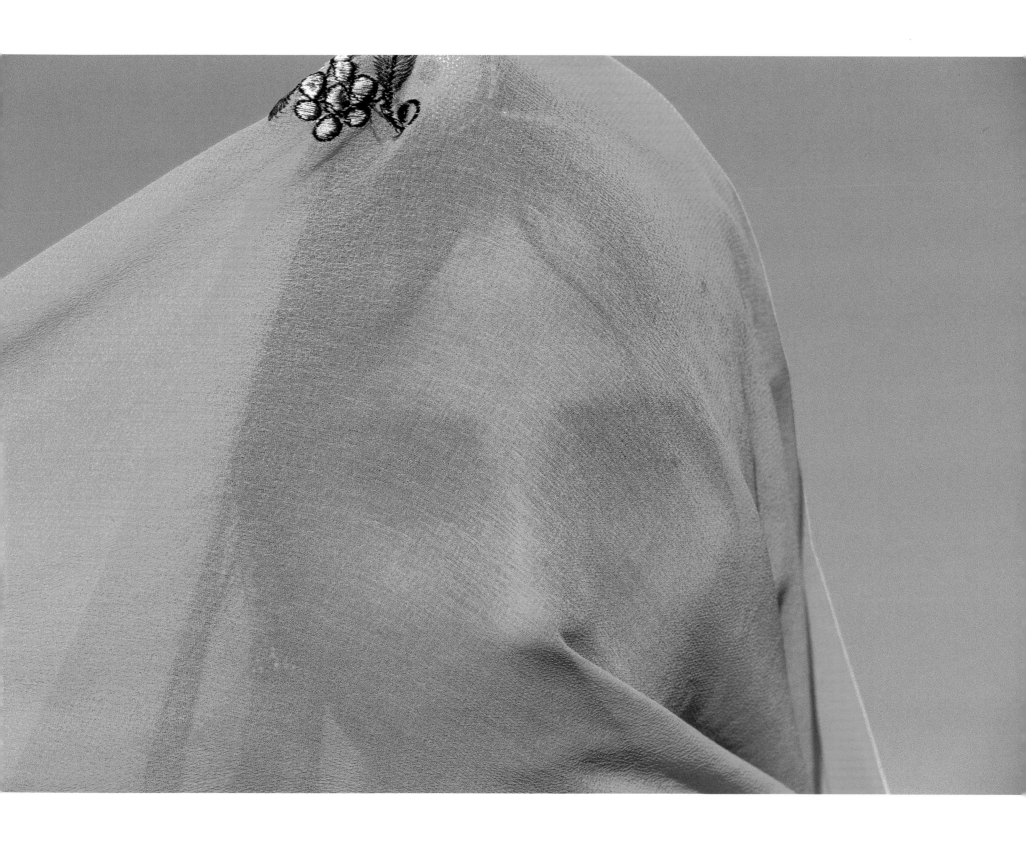

An elderly couple make their way to the temple on a cart drawn by other pilgrims.

A group of women huddle together at the marketplace in the pre-dawn chill.

Gypsy women and their children, in colourful traditional dress, wander across the dunes outside Pushkar.

Young women dressed in their most colourful saris and shawls gaze at Western visitors to the fair.

Rajasthani teenage girls enjoying the antics of a performing monkey at the fairground.

A boy performs a balancing act in exchange for a few rupees from passers-by.

Black and searing caverns where liquid metal makes eyes dance red in soot-stained faces; featureless plains where the parched earth groans as it cracks and buckles, where chemical reactions as insatiable as they are inexorable suck the very moisture from the air—this is a world of elements and elemental forces. Yet these are merely scenes from the workaday world for India's iron and salt workers, who labour in conditions even denizens of the industrial revolution's dark satanic mills would have found intolerable.

Around this vast nation, ancient iron smelters loom through their own pall: belching, roaring, breathing fire. Their hungry maws demand great chunks of ore to keep the red-hot lifeblood coursing. The workers scurry like ants, their limbs wiry and hard, as if the proximity to metal in its various states is, by some odd osmosis, slowly turning their own bones and flesh to iron. The older men move like they are beginning to rust.

Rusting, too, are the workers who move withered and whispering over the endless salt pans of the Little Rann of Kutch in western Gujurat. They produce millions of tonnes of salt each year—translucent cubes that appear as if by magic, like some invisible Picasso wielding his brush. The workers' cracked and scaly legs come to resemble the very earth they tread. It's hard to tell where flesh ends and the salt pan begins. By the time a salt-worker dies, his skin is so cured it won't even burn on his funeral pyre.

The glare of sun on salt quickly saps their vision. First their world turns black and white. Then, as cataracts turn their eyes to milky orbs, grim reality is day by day painted in softer focus. They say their thirst is unquenchable. As the monsoon abates and the sun turns merciless, conspiring with the growing accretions of crystals to steal every last drop of water, each breath rasps the throat like sandpaper.

Each day is like the last: the pans are raked, and the crystals tended. In the heat shimmer is a vista of impressions: bent, burnished backs raking and baking; anklets and nose rings glinting in the glare; flowing saris, a curve of hip, pots perched insouciantly atop heads.

Children's giggles emanate from within the scant shelter of thatched huts, the only shade for miles, and in between the clank and shudder of the pumps can be heard the resentful murmurs of the workers cursing mendacious traders.

Jason Gagliardi

Salt cakes the legs of a young boy in the Little Rann of Kutch.

When the monsoon abates, the workers pump underground water onto the saltpan, raking it over and over until the evaporation process leaves behind a carpet of crystals. The salt is then harvested under the searingly hot sun and taken to market, to be sold for a handful of rupees.

Bagging the 100-kilogram bags of salt and taking them to market is heavy work.

The teacher at the region's only school, Geeta Ben, is a 13-year-old with a third-grade education.

As well as labouring alongside the men in the salt pans, the women carry out a gruelling routine of daily chores, such as collecting firewood and water.

The salt workers and their families spend eight months of the year in huts made out of sticks, rice bags and straw.

Molten iron is poured by hand at a furnace in Chennai, southern India.

Only a few men still make steel by hand: it's hot, hard and dangerous work.

As well as bringing down blessings for kind weather and good crops, the annual monsoon festival in Osla
serves as a boisterous three-day matchmaking party for the young men and women of the village.

Osla, a speck of a village perched above an abyss in the Indian Himalayas, and a punishing seven-hour hike from the nearest road, is home to one of the last pockets of polyandry: the practice of taking more than one husband. Much rarer than polygamy, when a man takes more than one wife, polyandry existed among the ancient Britons and Arabs, as well as in India, Sri Lanka and Tibet. The practice was designed to prevent meagre inheritances from being carved up between family members, and to ensure that a woman and her children were cared for if one husband left the village in search of work or to fight a war.

The people of Osla trace their customs back to the Hindu epic *The Mahabharata,* in which the five heroic Pandava brothers are instructed by their mother Kunti to 'share whatever you have equally among all five of you.' When they realise she is talking about the affections of the beautiful Princess Draupadi, the brothers are aghast, but comply with their mother's wishes and share their bride.

Polyandry was outlawed in India in 1995, but despite the practice being condemned as backward and savage even by Osla's somewhat more worldly neighbours, the practical benefits ensure it survives.

When the price of land and the cost of a bride are at a premium, sharing a wife among several brothers means there is no need to divide the family's small plot, and there are fewer mouths to feed because less children are born into a family.

The settlement of some 100 simple dwellings is one of the most remote villages in the rugged region. It is this isolation that has allowed the practice to continue while nearby villages and towns lying closer to the highways are more influenced by the practices of the modern world. But even in Osla the men and women are under pressure to change their lifestyle.

'Tourism has definitely changed us,' says village headman Baru Singh. 'We're not backward anymore.'

The villagers quietly admit that despite the economic advantages, the unusual living arrangements can spark bitter jealousy and rows. Many believe their generation will be the last to practise polyandry. They hope that, one day, income from the recreational trekkers who are beginning to find their way here, as well as the earnings of relatives working in the plains, will enable future generations to stop sharing wives.

A young girl and her husbands, two brothers, make the long trek up to Osla.

Bana Devi with her two husbands, brothers Sulukh Ram (centre) and Salik, and their six children. No-one is sure which child is fathered by whom.

The POLYANDRISTS of OSLA

Women performing a tribal
dance at the monsoon festival.

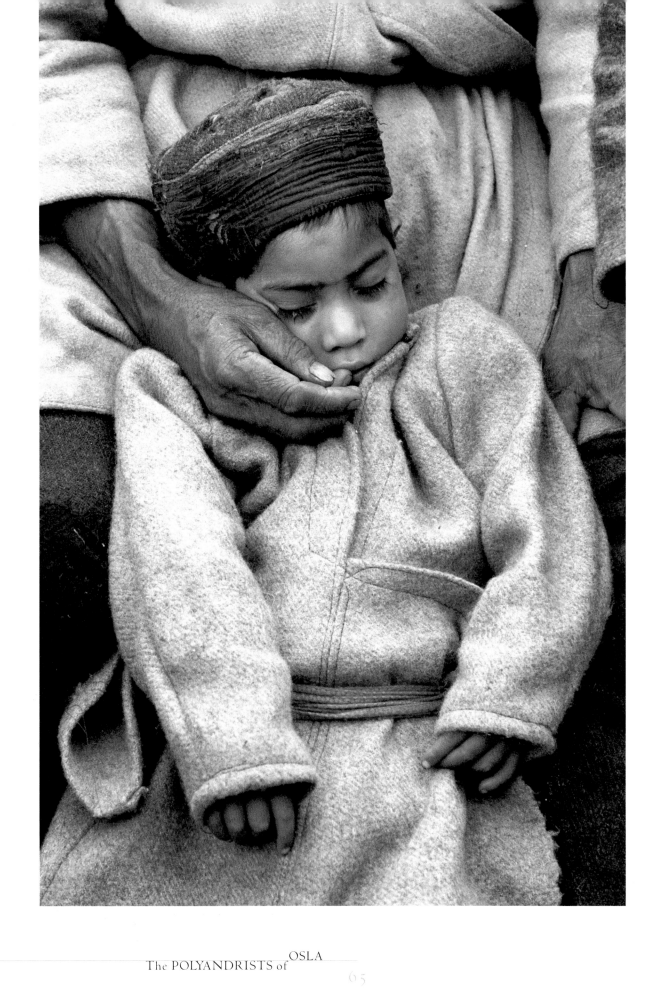

Most of the men from Osla work as coolies, heaving vegetables up and down the mountain ranges and portering for tourists.

Marina Beach is an unbroken stretch of sand that runs for 12 kilometres along the edge of Chennai, the southern city formerly known as Madras. Separated from the bustling city by a wide promenade and watched over by grand administrative buildings that date back to the British Raj, the world's second-longest beach is a haven for the city's residents, a magnet for street urchins and workers who come down for their morning wash, as well as joggers and well-to-do ladies who hold up their saris and dip their toes into the Bay of Bengal (few go any further; the waters are known for their fearful currents).

Many people visit Marina Beach to escape the dirt and noise of the big city, the confines of their communal homes and strict social rules. Young lovers come here to sit and hold hands, others find a quiet place to read a book, and children revel in the space to turn somersaults or fly paper kites. At night the beach turns into a fairground, where miniature hand-made ferris wheels are turned by hand and youngsters test their skill at the shooting stands. Wild looking men gallop up and down the shore offering rides on skinny ponies, and beggars man the promenade in search of a few spare rupees. As befits a city where snacking is an art form, vendors roast sweetcorn, served with salt, lime and chilli, and hot bhajis are lifted from vats of boiling oil set up on the sand and presented in a wrapping of dried leaves.

Dotted along the lawns of the promenade are a number of impeccably maintained statues of Tamil scholars, poets, patriots and personalities. First among them is the memorial to Mahatma Gandhi, father of the nation and leader of its struggle for freedom from the colonial yoke. Also honoured is Subash Chandra Bose, the Lion of Bengal, who led the Indian National Army against the British. But the colonialists also get a nod: a statue has been erected in remembrance of Sir Thomas Munro—a former governor who was known and respected in Chennai for his humanitarianism and sense of justice.

Marina is also a working beach, especially in the first few hours of the day. Buffalo are brought down to be washed in the surf, and fishermen set off to sea as they have done for hundreds of years. Early in the morning the city's housewives, as well as an army of maids from the middle-class suburbs, make their way down to the beach to buy fish for the lunch and dinner tables.

The fishermen, who have been working this stretch of the bay for generations, complain that stocks are running low and that they must venture out further each day if they want to fill their nets with anything other than plastic bags and water bottles. Wearing a simple white *dhoti* (loincloth) and a turban to keep off the sun, they head to sea before dawn, returning mid-morning, and make another trip in the afternoon. When the sun hangs overhead they retreat to the beachside huts where they live with their families. It's a tough life for these lean, strong men, but there's more money to be earned on the city beach than in the more tranquil fishing grounds elsewhere along the rugged coast of Tamil Nadu.

CHENNAI
MARINA BEACH

71

Marina Beach is where both rich and poor come to play, and one of the few places in Chennai where social and economic divides are forgotten.

CHENNAI
MARINA BEACH

73

While vendors walk the shoreline selling
flutes, snacks and toys, fishermen take a
break on the sand.

MARINA BEACH CHENNAI

Young men from the villages seize the chance to be photographed
with a cardboard cut-out of a famous Tamil movie star.

Fishermen have been working the seas off Marina Beach for hundreds of years, but today they must venture far from shore to find their catch.

HIDDEN FACES of INDIA

CHENNAI
MARINA BEACH

CHENNAI
MARINA BEACH

83

A young man and woman stroll along the beach on Valentine's Day, one of thousands of couples escaping the confines of their family homes.

CHENNAI
MARINA BEACH

85

Behind a curtain of fresh chillis, vegetable bhajis are lifted from vats of boiling oil, wrapped in dried leaves and served with a dollop of spicy chutney.

CHENNAI
MARINA BEACH

87

Ladakh: Land of the High Passes

On the northernmost tip of India, wedged between the Himalayas and the high-altitude Tibetan plateau, lies Ladakh. Its name literally means 'many passes' but the other terms used to describe it—Little Tibet, the Last Shangri-La, or Moon Land—equally conjure a sense of this most dramatic and desolate region of jagged mountain ranges, dry air and silent lakes. Because of its strategic location, next to Jammu and Kashmir over which Pakistan and India have fought three wars, Ladakh was closed to the outside world until 1974. Its borders with Pakistan and China are still disputed, making it an important military base for India.

Ladakh's capital, Leh, lies 3505 metres above sea level; high enough to leave new arrivals gasping for air when they stagger off the flight from Delhi. The flights that weave their way between the mountain tops before landing at the rudimentary airport can operate for only six months of the year, before encroaching snow and ice cut off this vital artery during the long, dark winter.

The harsh terrain is reflected in the lined faces of the people who eke out a living in this land. The Khampa nomads were the first to populate Ladakh, and in their brightly-coloured dress they still tend their yaks, sheep and goats on the high plateaus. The precious wool from these goats, known in the world's fashion capitals as pashmina, is sold by the merchants of Leh.

Ladakh is one of the last outposts of Tibetan Buddhism, within the embrace of predominantly Hindu India. However, the mosque at the hub of Leh's bazaar, dating back to the 17th century, and the Moravian Church, which was established in 1885, serve as prominent reminders of its mixed cultural heritage. Like most small Indian cities, Leh is changing fast as it attracts tourists and traders from all over the country. Natives of everywhere from coastal Goa to high-altitude Kashmir now call it home during the busy summer months.

A wizened gypsy woman walks along the road from Leh to Kargil in Kashmir. When asked her age, she replied with a smile, 'Who cares?'

An old man and his calf take a rest on the shores of beautiful Lake Tso Moriri, near the Tibetan border.

Archers from the Ladakhi village of Skurbuchan travel to Leh for the annual festival.

Monks travel to Leh to attend the annual festival.

HIDDEN FACES of INDIA

LAND of the HIGH PASSES
LADAKH

99

LAND of the HIGH PASSES

LADAKH

LAND of the HIGH PASSES

LADAKH

It was the largest gathering of humanity in the history of our planet. More than 80 million people, from every corner of India, gathered in the cold and the dust at Allahabad on the confluence of the three holy rivers: the Ganges, the Yamuna and the mythical Saraswati. United in an unshakeable belief in their religion, they bathed in the icy waters to wash away their sins and to gain salvation.

According to ancient Hindu mythology, the gods and the demons once fought a tremendous twelve-day battle for the *kumbh*—a pitcher containing the nectar of immortality. The god Vishnu captured the *kumbh* and spirited it away, but in his haste he spilt drops of the holy nectar onto Earth, at Allahabad, Haridwar, Nasik and Ujain.

The festival of Kumbh Mela has been taking place every three years for centuries, alternating between each of the four locations where the nectar fell, but the 'Maha' or 'Great' Kumbh Mela occurs only once every twelve years when a planetary alignment signals the start of one of the great pilgrimages on earth.

In *Following the Equator*, the great essayist Mark Twain wrote about the Kumbh Mela he witnessed in 1896. The sights he records are uncannily similar to those of modern-day Kumbh Melas.

On a long curved spit between the rivers, towns of tents were visible, with a multitude of fluttering pennons, and a mighty swarm of pilgrims. It was a troublesome place to get down to, and not a quiet place when you arrived; but it was interesting. There was a world of activity and turmoil and noise, partly religious, partly commercial; for the Mohammedans were there to curse and sell, and the Hindoos to buy and pray. It is a fair as well as a religious festival. Crowds were bathing, praying, and drinking the purifying waters, and many sick pilgrims had come long journeys in palanquins to be healed of their maladies by a bath; or if that might not be, then to die on the blessed banks and so make sure of heaven.

There were fakeers in plenty, with their bodies dusted over with ashes and their long hair caked together with cow-dung; for the cow is holy and so is the rest of it; so holy that the good Hindoo peasant frescoes the walls of his hut with this refuse, and also constructs ornamental figures out of it for the gracing of his dirt floor. There were seated families, fearfully and wonderfully painted, who by attitude and grouping represented the families of certain great gods. There was a holy man who sat naked by the day and by the week on a cluster of iron spikes, and did not seem to mind it; and another holy man, who stood all day holding his withered arms motionless aloft, and was said to have been doing it for years. All of these performers have a cloth on the ground beside them for the reception of contributions, and even the poorest of the people give a trifle and hope that the sacrifice will be blessed to him. At last came a procession of naked holy people marching by and chanting, and I wrenched myself away.

Pilgrims, in their millions, arrive for the festival.

An elderly woman helps another in
the morning mist of the Ganges.

MAHA KUMBH MELA²⁰⁰¹

An initiation ceremony for new sadhus (religious ascetics) at the banks of the Yamuna River.

MAHA KUMBH MELA ^{2001}

111

A 70-year-old Baba, or
holy man, who was born
without arms or legs. His
followers consider him to
be a living god.

Sadhus line up at the confluence of the Ganges and Yamuna rivers, waiting to immerse themselves in the icy waters.

Ash-covered sadhus after their morning dip in the holy rivers.

Hundreds of boats ferry pilgrims to the confluence of the Yamuna and Ganges rivers, considered the most sacred spot to bathe.

The White Sikhs of Amritsar

It's three in the morning at the Miri Piri Academy at Amritsar, and bleary-eyed American kids with buckets are sluicing the hallowed marble *parikrama*, or walkway, of one of India's most sacred places. The gilded domes of the Golden Temple of Amritsar shimmer above the 'pool of nectar', and the voices of priests reciting scriptures drift across the water. From the reservoir, the buckets pass along a chain of hands as the children perform their regular *seva*, or duty. These young Americans are being raised here at Amritsar, the home of the Sikhs, in a unique tradition that stretches back to the 17th century in the Punjab.

'Back home people stare at us because of our turbans. In India they stare at us because we're white,' says one of the students.

An orthodox Sikh must conform with the 'Five Ks'. Their hair (*kesh*) is believed to be a source of strength and is never cut; instead unruly locks are bundled into turbans. Sikhs must also wear a bangle (*kara*), breeches (*katcha*) and carry a comb (*kangha*) and dagger (*kirpan*). This distinctive dress declares their identity and devotion to their religion. In the fast-paced modern world only a minority of Sikhs still follow every such article of faith, but the Miri Piri Academy is not only keeping the tradition alive, but also spreading it across the world. Here, foreign students—boys and girls alike— wear the turban and carry small ceremonial daggers.

The students start their day at the temple, or with strenuous yoga or quiet meditation. After breakfast and assembly the school's grounds echo with the clash of staves as the students practice *gatka*. The early Sikhs had to take up arms to defend their beliefs against the older and much larger Hindu and Muslim communities, and this fluid sword-fighting style allowed the outnumbered Sikhs to survive in India, and to become useful allies of the British Raj in suppressing rebellions at home and crushing the Empire's enemies abroad. At Miri Piri, sword fighting is merely a novel form of exercise; a relief from the complexities of turban-tying.

The Academy was started by Harbhajan Singh Khalsa, a Sikh immigrant to the United States who, while teaching yoga in the 1960s, discovered that his students also hungered for new spiritual disciplines as well. Today's Miri Piri pupils are the children of those first converts. For eight months a year they live in a cloistered environment, at arm's length from contemporary American culture, but on the fringes of Indian society as well. Their uniform is an eclectic mix of Western sneakers and the Punjabi *bana*, or tunic, and their dorms are plastered with posters of rock idols. Not all the students are sure they will uphold orthodox Sikhism once their education is over, but the challenge of staying different will be with them throughout their lives.

Christopher Kremmer

Aftar Kaur, a 12-year-old from New Mexico, holds a heavy iron sabre at arm's length until the pain becomes unbearable.

The WHITE SIKHS of AMRITSAR

Students rise at 2.30 am to scrub the marble *parikrama*, or walkway, surrounding the sacred pool of the Golden Temple.

The WHITE SIKHS of AMRITSAR

The WHITE SIKHS of AMRITSAR

129

A boy saunters to breakfast in sneakers
and a turban.

Sport and dance—a fusion of two
cultures at the Miri Piri Academy.

A quick snooze on the bus that takes students to the Golden Temple for early morning prayers.

The WHITE SIKHS of AMRITSAR

The WHITE SIKHS of AMRITSAR

It's an unlikely battleground, this broad, sacred river rolling confidently towards the Arabian Sea between the Satpudas and Vindhyas ranges. But along the banks of the Narmada, India's longest westward-flowing river, the riverine communities fight to save their civilization. For fifteen years they have waged a Gandhian struggle to prevent the inundation of the valley and its mainly tribal populace of some 25 million people.

At the tiny village of Domkhedi, a clutch of thatched huts nestling in the cornfields within sight of the river, each hut flies the blue flag of the Narmada Bachao Andolan. The NBA is leading the struggle against the Sardar Sarovar Dam, a concrete wall more than a kilometre wide that will block the river, submerge the villages and displace tens of thousands of people.

This year, a poor monsoon has saved Domkhedi. The failed rains have postponed the submergence for another year, so the scruffy village survives as a base camp for the non-violent resistance. Yet this war already has its casualties. In 1999, a seven-year-old girl, Lata Vasave, died a horrible death, stuck in the silt beds which have become deeper and more treacherous since construction of the dam began. Nobody heard her screams as they subsided into the mud. A river that has sustained life for thousands of years has become, through man's intervention, a death trap.

In June, the residents of nearby Jalsindhi were surprised by a visit from their postman, who usually sits 20 kilometres away waiting to meet travellers to the village, rather than making the arduous journey along the forest paths himself. The postman carried disturbing news in the form of a government notice, in Hindi, to Gulabia Shankar, a 40-year-old farmer whose land fronts the

Narmada. Gulabia, like most of his neighbours, is illiterate, so a friend read the letter to him. 'You are warned that your home might be submerged. If there are any homes below this level, we request you to inform them', it said. The authorities are legally bound to give a year's notice of submergence, but for Gulabia a few weeks was considered sufficient. 'Villages have been drowned without the inhabitants even being informed, let alone being offered or provided with any alternatives', says Joe Athialy, a postgraduate from Kerala who has worked full-time for the NBA since 1994.

So came the flood tide, rising inexorably towards Gulabia's home. Then, when half his land was submerged, it halted. An act of God, maybe, but half the land means half the food with which to feed Gulabia's wife and eight children. A typically handsome Bhil tribesman sporting a tattooed forehead and wispy beard, Gulabia is lean and cheerful, except when the conversation turns to Narmada. He's not shifting. 'There is no point thinking about leaving,' he says, 'because what the government is offering is simply not practical.' His words echo the stubborn defiance of the entire village.

Next year, perhaps, the rest of Gulabia's land will disappear beneath these unnatural waters, but life continues as it must. In the family's spacious home, flour is still ground under a heavy round stone set on a teak base, a device nowadays considered an objet d'art for middle-class Indian homes. The great displacement of millions from the land to the urban fringes is creating a flood of antiques. Until their turn comes, Gulabia's sons play flutes fashioned from bamboo, and his body-jewelled daughters wash their hair in buttermilk.

Christopher Kremmer

Two women collect water at the river settlement of Domkhedi.

The goddess Narmada Devi stands guard at the entrance to the tiny riverside village of Domkhedi.

This land was Bhaji Bhai's farm before the government built a giant canal through it to feed water into the dam.

Gulabia Shankar's daughters, Usha Ben and Sauithi Ben, stand where their father's farm used to be, before the dam waters rose.

Hindus believe that to bathe in the Ganges washes away their sins, but merely to look at the Narmada has the same result.

VALLEY
NARMADA

After losing their jobs in the jungles of Asia, where for centuries they hauled away precious loads of teak and mahogany, domesticated elephants have unceremoniously joined the ranks of the unemployed. There are now some 16 000 in Asia, living everywhere from sanctuaries to city streets; many reduced to performing tricks for tourists or begging from passers-by. But in some remote pockets, like the logging camp in Thunakadavo, on the border of Kerala and Tamil Nadu in southern India, their traditional working life continues. And in the tiny and isolated community of a dozen families on Senakadavo Hill live some of the last of the mahouts.

'God has given us the task of looking after these animals. That is the reason why we are here. This is not a job like being a conductor in a bus. This is our duty,' says the oldest of the mahouts, 65-year-old A. Palani. 'We have been with these animals since birth. We live with them, work with them and sleep with them. This is a relationship like that between father and son. Sometimes we get on and other times we give them a couple of slaps to get them back to where they should be.'

A. Palani was born in Senakadavo and learned the trade of caring for and working with elephants from his father, finally taking over from him in 1963. During those long years he has cared for just three elephants and he speaks of each as one might a close family member.

The gods have been good to A. Palani—he has six sons. But to his great sadness only one has decided to become a mahout; the others have all left for the cities. He fears that as the bright lights lure the young men of this village, and others like it, the art of working with elephants will be lost forever. Although he is now preparing for his retirement, A. Palani hopes that by staying on in the logging camp in his old age he can help preserve the legacy.

'I will pass on my knowledge to the young,' he says. 'Some will listen and others will not. Humans are just like elephants in so many ways. Not all can be mahouts. You have to make sure you teach the ones with brains because the elephants will soon find out you have none and then the story will be different,' he laughs.

'To understand an elephant and to gain the respect of the animal you have to spend time with them; become one with them. You cannot learn to be a mahout by going to school or reading about it in a book. You have to go into the forest with them. Most of the youngsters now would rather go to town and go to the late movies. What will happen to these elephants after we die?'

Here as in every other country along the Ivory Crescent, a broad swathe of Asia where wild elephants once roamed in great numbers while their domesticated brothers and sisters laboured in the jungles, there is no clear future for the great beasts.

'They will become old like me and get moved into the city to a different life,' says A. Palani. 'These are the changing times and we are the last who are living with them.'

With a skill honed through years of practice, an elephant deftly clears away a fallen tree.

A mahout family awakens to begin another day caring for the elephants.

In a mahout village, knowledge is passed down from generation to generation.

Kumar and his daughter Vina wrap up against the morning chill at the mahout camp.

Twice a day, loaves of oat flour and brown sugar are baked and fed to the elephants, helping to strengthen the bond between man and beast.

A. Palani, the oldest mahout in the village.

My deepest gratitude to Christopher and Janaki Kremmer for their wisdom and hospitality;

to my wife Sarah and my parents for their endless support; to the many friends who encouraged me;

and, of course, to all the people who appear in this book.

First published in Australia in 2002 by
New Holland Publishers (Australia) Pty Ltd
Sydney • Auckland • London • Cape Town

14 Aquatic Drive Frenchs Forest NSW 2086 Australia
218 Lake Road Northcote Auckland New Zealand
86 Edgware Road London W2 2EA United Kingdom
80 McKenzie Street Cape Town 8001 South Africa

Copyright © 2002 photographs: Palani Mohan
Copyright © 2002 text: Palani Mohan; Christopher Kremmer; Jason Gagliardi (as credited)
Copyright © 2002 New Holland Publishers (Australia) Pty Ltd

National Library of Australia Cataloguing-in-Publication Data:

Mohan, Palani
Hidden Faces of India

ISBN 1 86436 751 2.

1. India — Pictorial works. 2. India — Description and travel. I. Title.

915.4

Publishing Manager: Anouska Good
Project Editor: Sophie Church
Designer: Nanette Backhouse
Production Manager: Janelle Treloar
Reproduction: Colourscan, Singapore
Printer: Everbest Printing, China

This book was shot on Kodak film.

Kodak Professional